MMA Foundations

Volume 1

by Elijah Stevenson

MMA Foundations

ISBN: 978-0-6454395-0-2 (paperback)

© 2021 by Elijah Stevenson

All Rights Reserved

Photography by Dean Russel

Cover Design and Layout by Jason Rennie

No part of this book may be reproduced, stored in a retrieval system of transmitted by any means without the written permission of the author.

Table of Contents

What to put in your training bag	7
Stance and Movement	9
Striking Basics	13
Punches	25
Blocking	35
Evading	41
Grips	47
Positions	52
Solo Basics	62
Submissions	96
Take Downs	128
Take Downs	128
MMA 8	139
Fitness	158
Fitness	158
Index	189

Dedicated to my Daughter
Sienna Catherine Stevenson
Daddy loves you so much

What to put in your training bag

What to put in your training bag

Before you start training at home or at a gym begin to acquire the training equipment you will need.

WHAT TO PUT IN YOUR TRAINING BAG

EQUIPMENT
- Skipping rope

FIRST AID
- Band aids
- Bandage

HYGIENE
- Nail clippers
- Deodorant
- Training towel

PROTECTIVE
- Head gear
- Mouth guard
- Chest guard (for women)
- Groin guard (for men)
- Shin Guards
- 4-6oz MMA Gloves (finger-less)
- 10-16oz Boxing Gloves
- Hand Wraps

Stance and Movement

Your stance and how you move from point A to point B may be different depending on the style of martial arts you choose

Stance and Movement

MMA STANCE

The MMA stance is the perfect all round stance. Its square base makes it suitable to shoot for take downs or sprawl to defend them. The hands are usually high for striking defence and hips facing forward for checking leg kicks.

JIU-JITSU & WRESTLING STANCE

The forward facing wrestling stance is like the MMA stance to shoot for and defend take downs.

Keeping the hands either low in its low stance or a hand facing up and a hand facing down to gain a tactical advantage.

Stance and Movement

SHORT BLADED STANCE

With a short bladed stance to create less of a target the hands stay high and elbows are close to the body to protect against body shots.
This stance tends to be lacking in defense for low kicks and take downs. Typically used for short range.

MUAY THAI

A forward facing squared stance that is light on the lead foot to check kicks and return teeps quickly and efficiently.
Hands stay high to protect from strikes and trap opponents hands as a defensive tactic.

Stance and Movement

LONG BLADED STANCE

With a short bladed stance to create less of a target the hands stay high and elbows are close to the body to protect against body shots.
This stance tends to be lacking in defense for low kicks and take downs.
Typically used for long range.

Striking Basics

Striking Basics

Before we start kicking and punching each other it is important to know what strikes you will be performing and how to use them properly

Striking Basics

FRONT PUSH KICK

- Starting in your preferred stance chamber your kick by lifting your knee up and pulling your toes back to your shin

- With the FLAT of your foot push your opponent back by thrusting your hips forward and leaning back.

- Return to your chambered position referred to in step 1

Striking Basics

Striking Basics

STABBING FRONT KICK

- Starting in your preferred stance chamber your kick by lifting your knee up and pulling your toes back to your shin

- With the BALL of your foot push your opponent back by thrusting your hips forward and leaning back.

- Return to your chambered position referred to in step 1

Striking Basics

Striking Basics

ROUND HOUSE BAT

- Thrust your hips forwards to push your knee towards your target

- Point your toes to engage your leg muscles and ligaments

- Propelling your arm backwards will assist in creating power, balance and a harder target to counter.

Striking Basics

Striking Basics

Striking Basics

ROUND HOUSE SNAP

- Start by chambering your preferred kicking leg

- Extend your leg making contact with the instep where your foot meets your shin

- Bring your kick back to the chamber and return it back to the ground

Striking Basics

Striking Basics

KNEES

- Thrust your hips forwards to push your knee towards your target

- Point your toes to engage your leg muscles and ligaments

- Propelling your arm backwards will assist in creating power, balance and a harder target to

Striking Basics

Striking Basics

Punches

First we learn how to make a fist then we learn how to use them going through the fundamental punching techniques is cruciall for your MMA journey

Striking Basics

MAKING A FIST

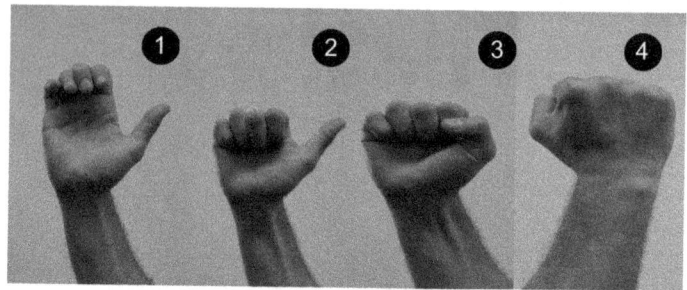

- With an open hand close fist each knuckle at a time

- Once your hand is completely closed place your thumb on the first finger

- Placing the thumb on the second or third finger will destabilise your wrist causing injury

- By squeezing your thumb you should feel your forearm muscles tense creating a strong foundation for your wrist support

- When making contact with your fist aim to strike with the top knuckles of the pointer and middle fingers only.

- Punching with the lower three knuckles may cause injuries such as boxers fracture.

Striking Basics

JAB

- Extend your lead hand in a straight line towards your target

- Keep your elbows in tight to your body to reduce any telegraphing

- Turn your fist palm down just before contact to strike with your top 2 knuckles

PRO TIP
By lifting the heel of your lead foot as you punch you can generate more power and speed.

Striking Basics

Striking Basics

CROSS

- Extend yourt rear hand in a straight line towards your target

- Keep your elbows in tight toy our body to reduce any telegraphing

- Point your rear toes to your target and your shin to the ground to aid in turning your hips over

- Turn your fist palm down just before contact to strike with your top 2 knuckles

Striking Basics

Striking Basics

HOOK

- Push your lead toes into the ground turn your hips and body inwards

- Simultaneously lift your elbow as your body twisting propels your fist in a hooking motion

- Punching past the centre line keeping your chin protected by keeping it tucked behind your shoulder

Striking Basics

THE GREAT DEBATE
THUMB UP OR THUMB DOWN

For short range hooks keep your thumb up pointing towards the sky
For mid range turn your thumb towards you
As for long range turn it down to the ground, note this will begin to look like an overhand strike at this point.
The reason for doing this is to ensure that upon contact you are still striking with the top two knuckles of your fist.

Striking Basics

UPPER CUT

- Without dropping your hand low extend it slightly towards your opponent

- Push off your rear foot to thrust your punch towards you target

- Punch through your intended target to cause the most damage

Striking Basics

Blocking

Blocking

It is import to know how to react when someone is striking you. Now we wil go through your basic blocking princples.

Blocking

HIGH GUARD

Keeping both arms and hands in close and up high protecting the head. This defensive guard is a useful tool for protecting yourself from aggressive fighters that head hunt. This is especially strong for straight attacks by bringing both your forearms together creates a strong shield like formation. Being a high guard this can leave you at a disadvantage for lower attacks if you are not careful.

PARRY

A slight tap to change the incoming directory of a straight punch like a jab or a cross. It is important not push your opponents hand down to the ground or away as it will leave you open for a counter. A slight tap is all it takes to change the line of fire.

Blocking

HOOK BLOCK

Commonly referred to as answering the phone or combing your hair, when done correctly your arms will take the brunt of the impact as your opponent throws a hook punch. It is crucial to tuck your chin behind your shoulder as you brace for impact. Gripping the base of the skull just behind the ear to protect the more vulnerable parts of your neck.

BODY BLOCK

Keeping your hands attached to your chin just as you would in high guard touch your desired elbow to your hip bone to protect your floating ribs, liver and other vulnerable areas of the abdomen. It is a very common mistake to drop your hands from your chin from being to stiff to move in this way, try relaxing by taking a deep breath and and allowing your body to move in the way it wants to.

Blocking

OVERHAND BLOCK

This may look as if your just waving to a friend or signalling for someone to stop what they are doing, if so that is completely correct. The only difference is when you say stop you are strong, using this block as a strike forearm to forearm as the overhand punch is delivered. Forearm conditioning can be very advantagous as some traditionanal martial arts have demonstrated for centuries.

UPPERCUT BLOCK

Blocking the Uppercut can be quiet simple especially from the high guard. The uppercuts trajectory comes under the chin and usallly to the centreline of the body. By drawing your elbow across your chest pass the centreline of your body this will prevent the punch coming under your guard. Both blocks will block either the left or right uppercut although blocking the mirrored side can be more adavntagious if they are throwing more punches after.

Blocking

LEG CHECK

Lifting your knee out to a 45 degree angle with your shin facing the low kick. Pulling them back to your shins creating a hook you prepare your muscles, ligiments and tendons for impact. As you recieve the low kick to your shin allow your leg to absorb the kick by bringing it back towards yourself then kicking your leg back out to throw the attackers leg back towards them. Checking the kick with this absorbing and pushing technique will midigate the damadge you would normally recieve by checking with a strong wall shin to shin.

Blocking

3 POINT BLOCK

The 3 point block is used to defend roundhouse head kick. By spreading the impact across 3 points of impact the bicep, the forearm and the hand. Just like the Hook block "answer the phone" and simaltaniously catch the shin with your hand, moving towards the kick will jam the power.

Evading

Evading

MMA is the art of hitting and not getting hit. It is always a good idea to get out of the way of an incoming attack

Evading

SLIPPING

Slipping straight punches is crucial in MMA. To slip a punch bring your head approximately 6 inches (more if your gloves are bigger) off the centre line to narrowly miss the punch. Your head should not go so far it passes the knee, this will result in a loss of balance. It is also important to keep both hands on your chin as you slip the punches.

Evading

PULL

Stepping your rear leg back allows a greater range of motion as you pull your head away from head kicks and incoming head attacks

Evading

WEAVING

Rolling or "weaving" hook punches start exactly as if your are slipping your head off the centre line away from the hook. This will allow you to roll with the punch if they do hit you.
Secondly with your eyes on your opponent duck just under the punch and circle back to your upright position

Evading

Evading

FRAME AND EVADE

The frame and evade is used to dodge low kicks and nullify any hand attacks that may follow. Simply place hands outwards on to the gloves off your opponent and pull you legs back and together and allow the kick to swing by. Now return back to your fighting stance

Grips

Grips

Learning how to grip and hold your opponent is a valuable skill to master, along with which grip for what scenario

Grips

3 FINGER HOLD

By gripping the 3 fingers the pinky, the ring and the middle finger you create a strong grip perfect for clinching your opponent even when sweat begins to make things a bit slippery.

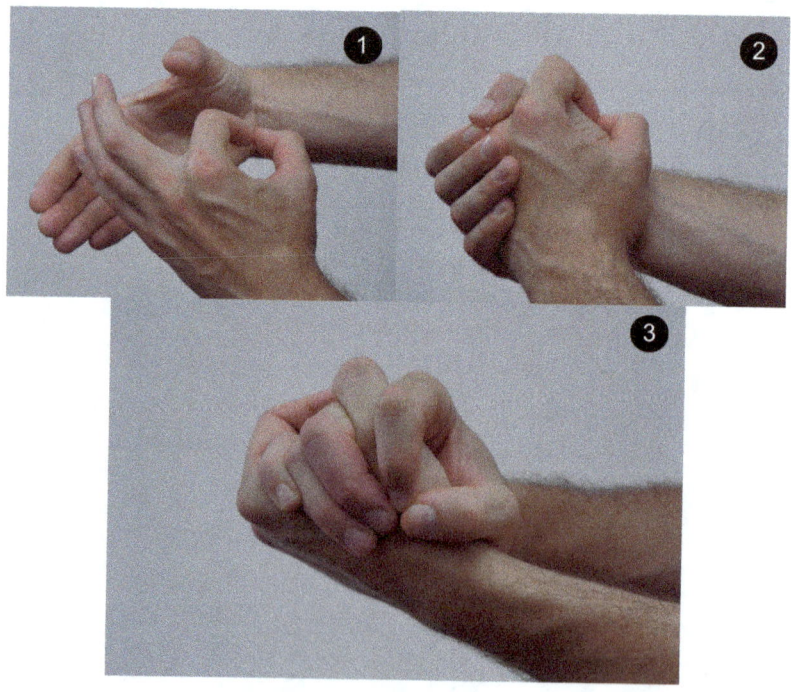

Grips

GABBLE GRIP

The Gabble Grip is one of the strongest grips. By clasping the hands together ensuring thumbs are not interlocked as it diminishes the strength of the grip.the down side to this grip is the mobility and flection is not that great.

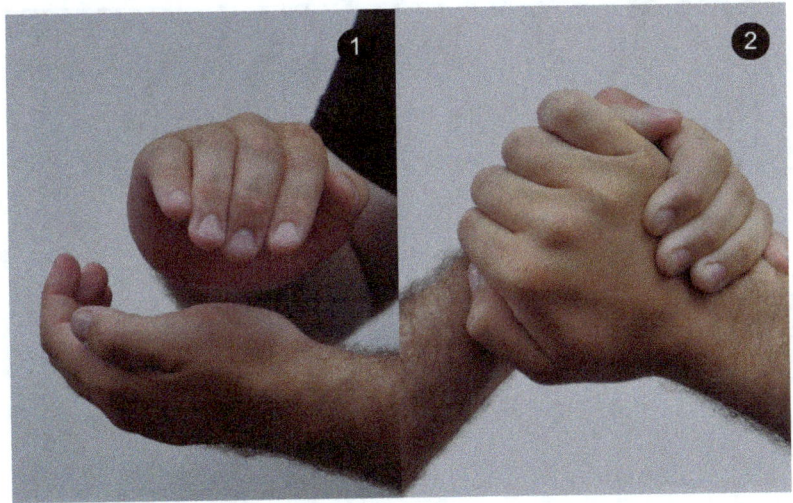

Grips

S GRIP

Creating 2 hooks that interlock, the S grips strength lies in the mobility and flection of the hold. Use of this grip is common when fighting larger opponents as it give you a little more reach and is a suitable substitute for the gabble grip

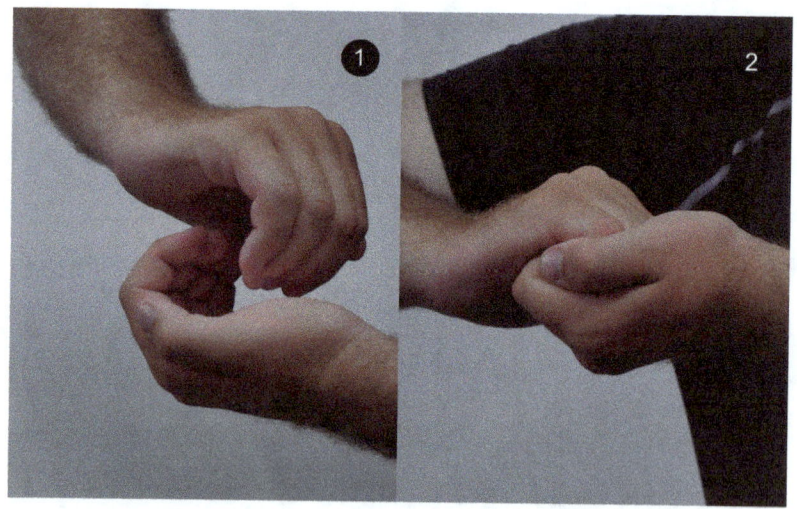

Grips

BALL & SOCKET GRIP

By grabbing your wrist and with a slight bend you create a strong grip commonly used for submissions like the guillotine. Called the ball and socket grip due to the hands resemblance to just that

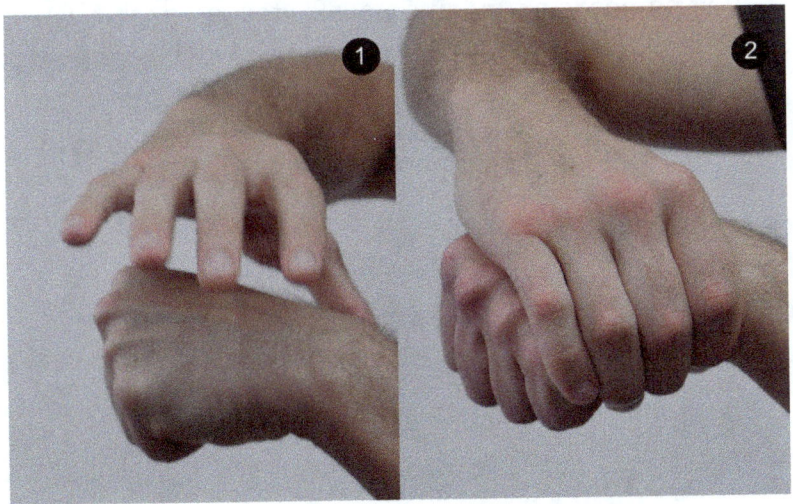

Postions

Positions

Understanding the different postions ont he ground and their names is a fundamental skill to lean as this will shorten the learning time and help you to pick things up quicker.
Knowing the terminology will save you and your coach time as they will not have to explain what it means to "Jump into mount" for example.

Postions

OPEN GUARD

In this position you lay on your back with your opponent between your legs and your feet unlocked and agile to prevent your opponent passing into a advantageous position

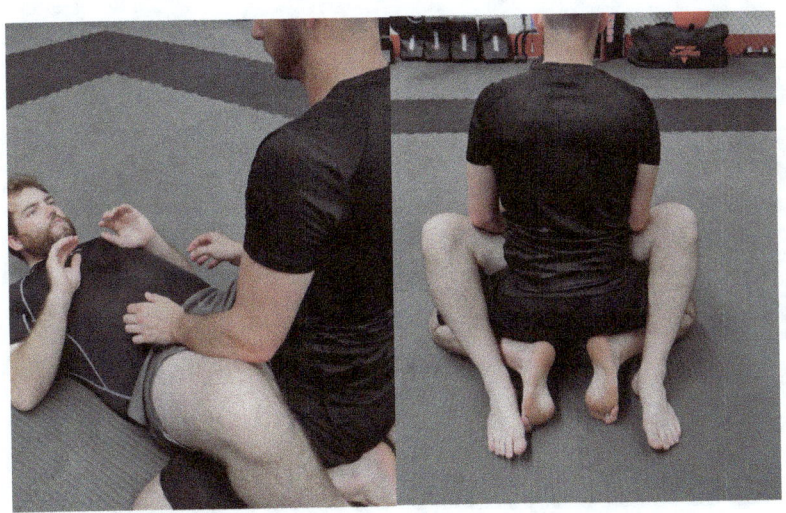

Postions

CLOSED GUARD

Akin to "OPEN GUARD" the same foundation arises. The main difference your feet are interlocked creating a stronger more restrained guard. Extending your legs you create distance between you and your opposition, bringing your knees to your chest you bring them in close. This is a great distance management tool.

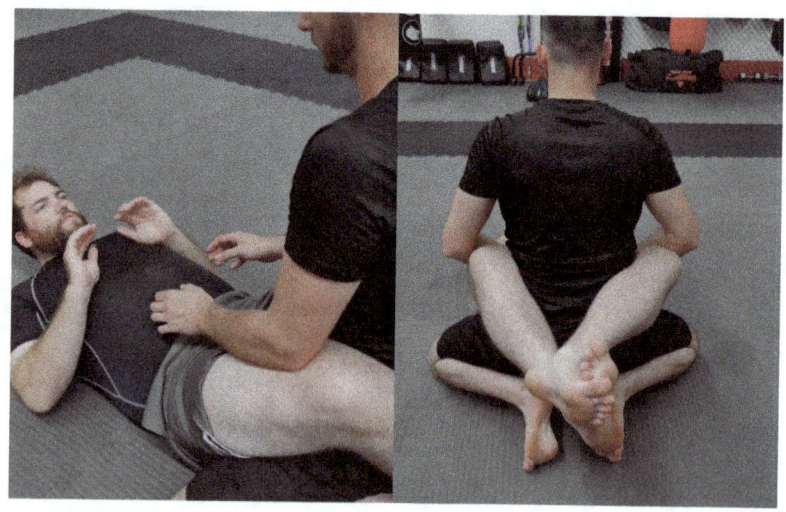

Postions

CROOKED GUARD

Crooked guard or commonly refereed to as the pre triangle just as the name implies it is similar to open and closed guard except in this case one leg is over the shoulder and one is under. This is a advantage position because of its entry to many submissions. Maintaining head control will prevent them from standing up.

Postions

HALF GUARD

The half guard position requires locking one leg between your own from the guarded position it is wise to not let your opponent pass all the way through into a full mount. A large advantage to this position is that a high percent of sweeps are completed from this position.

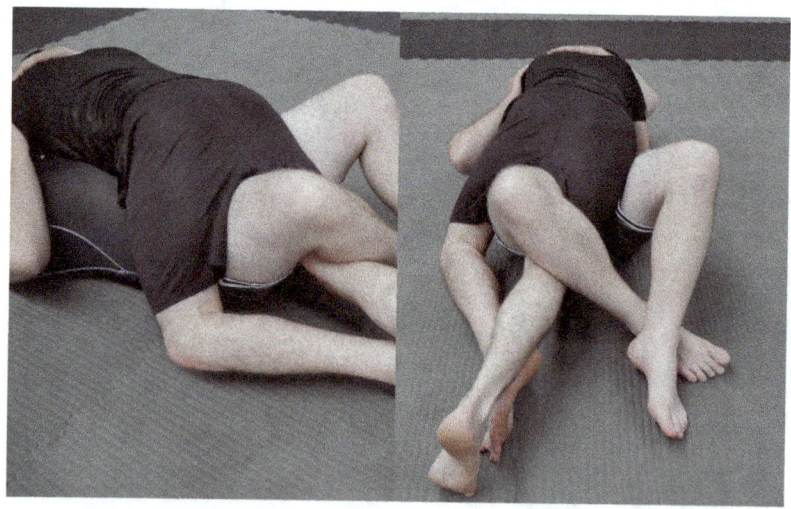

Postions

KNEE ON BELLY

A very uncomfortable position when on the bottom of this technique. The knee weighs down on the belly and/or the chest making it harder to breath for your opponent. It is important to control their shoulders by pushing them down this prevents them from rolling in or out.

Postions

MOUNT

The mounted position is a very dominate place to win in exchanges. Sitting high up on the chest pinning the shoulders down you create all kinds of problems for your opponent. It is key to stay up high on the chest and not towards the hips as they can bump their hips up throwing you off balance.

Postions

SCARF HOLD

Gripping under both triceps with the inner leg out towards the head and the outer leg posted up and out to a 45 degree angle. Keep your weight heavy on their chest by lifting your hips off the ground.

SIDE CONTROL

Bring both of your knees to your opponent, 1 on the hip and the other up high towards the shoulder. Bring your top hand under the head then grip it with your other hand. By keeping your sternum lower than theirs it will create a heavier side control for them to defend against

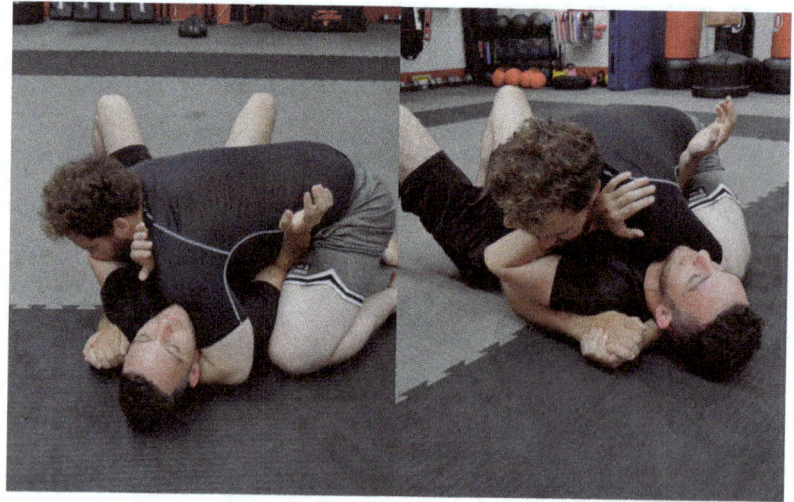

TACTICAL MOUNT

As the opponent is on their side 1 leg comes behind and along the back and the other in front posted up and brought in tight. This prevents any rolling in or out of the tactical mount. An additional set up you can add is the "GIFT WRAP" performed by pulling their top arm around their head and pulling it through as if they were choking themselves.

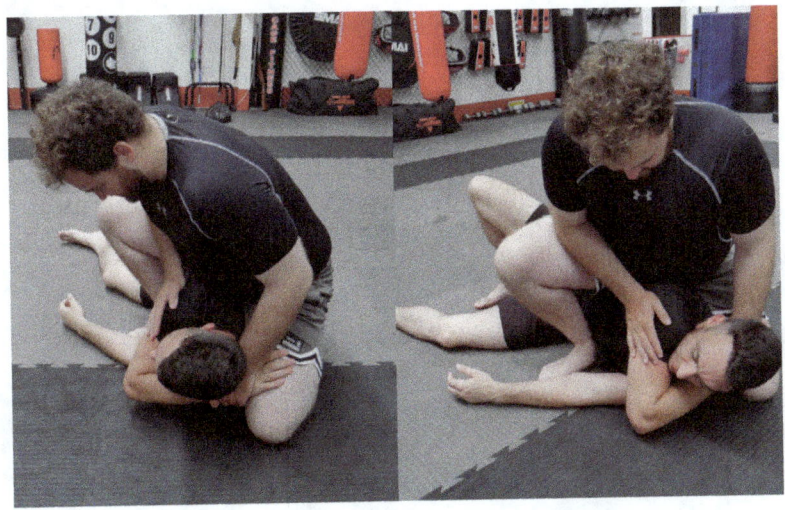

Solo Basics

Mastering the solo basics will help build a strong foundation for your wrestling and Jiu Jitsu. Exact technique that you practice helps train your body to move with proper technique in your training with or without a partner

Solo Basics

BASE STANDUPS

From a fight stance place 1 knee at a time down to the ground, sit down as wide and as low as you can to create and strong base. Keeping your toes active as seen in the photo. Then stand back up 1 leg at a time and repeat.

Solo Basics

Solo Basics

BRIDGE TURNOVER

- Laying on your back bring your feet right up to your hips and face them out on a 45 degree angle whilst keeping your arms in tight to your body.

- Push your hips as high as you can to the back off the room and look over your shoulder to begin to roll at a 45 degree angle behind you.

- Complete the transition through until you are on your forearms and knees. Reset and repeat on opposite side

Solo Basics

Solo Basics

Solo Basics

HIP ESCAPE

- Laying on your back bring your feet right up to your hips and face them out on a 45 degree angle whilst keeping your arms in tight to your body.

- Push off your hips to the back of the room and come up onto the side of your hips in an explosive movement as you try and reach for your toes.

- Realign your body and reset, now repeat on the opposite side

Solo Basics

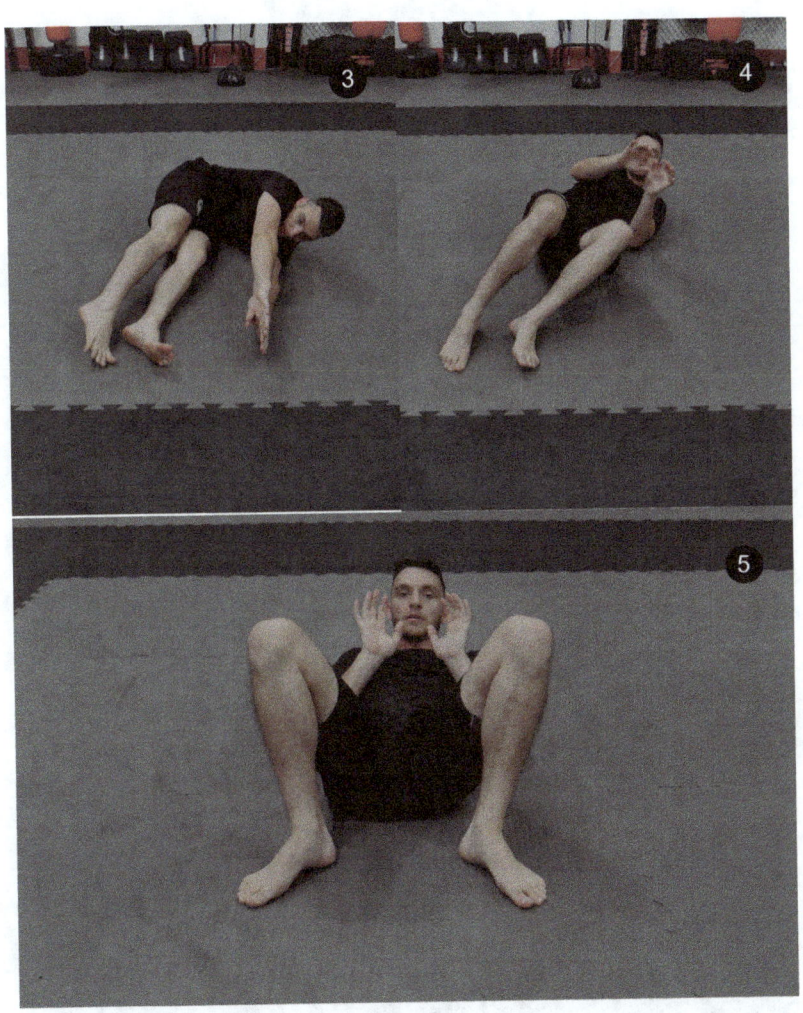

Solo Basics

SHOOT

- From your fight stance change you level by bending your knees and keep your back straight

- Keep your arms in tight and lower your front knee to the ground

- Bring your rear leg to the front and reset and repeat on the other side

Solo Basics

Solo Basics

SPRAWL

- Start by placing your hands on the ground
- With your hands in place throw your legs back off to an angle
- Lower your hips down to the ground
- Jump up promptly and repeat the sprawl on different angles

Solo Basics

Solo Basics

TACTICAL STAND UP

- Start in a sitting position with one leg posted the other laid down

- Your front hand in front as a buffer for incoming attacks and the rear hand posted supporting you

- Lift your hips off the ground by posting up with your rear hand and front leg

- Bring the other leg right back maintaining the buffer between you and your opponent

- This ensures you move backwards away from danger

Solo Basics

Transitions

BACK ESCAPE

- Once your opponent has taken your back and immediately scoot your hips down and away, simultaneously tuck your chin down, bring your shoulders up pulling their arms in and down to prevent any chokes.

- Bring your feet right up to your towards your hips to relieve any strength they have in their hooks (legs)

- Tuck your elbows in between your body and their knees

- Scoop your arms all the way through under their knees

- Lean back and lift your arms in the air forcing them to fall backwards

- 6. Follow your opponent turning into them and scramble for positio

Transitions

Transitions

Transitions

Transitions

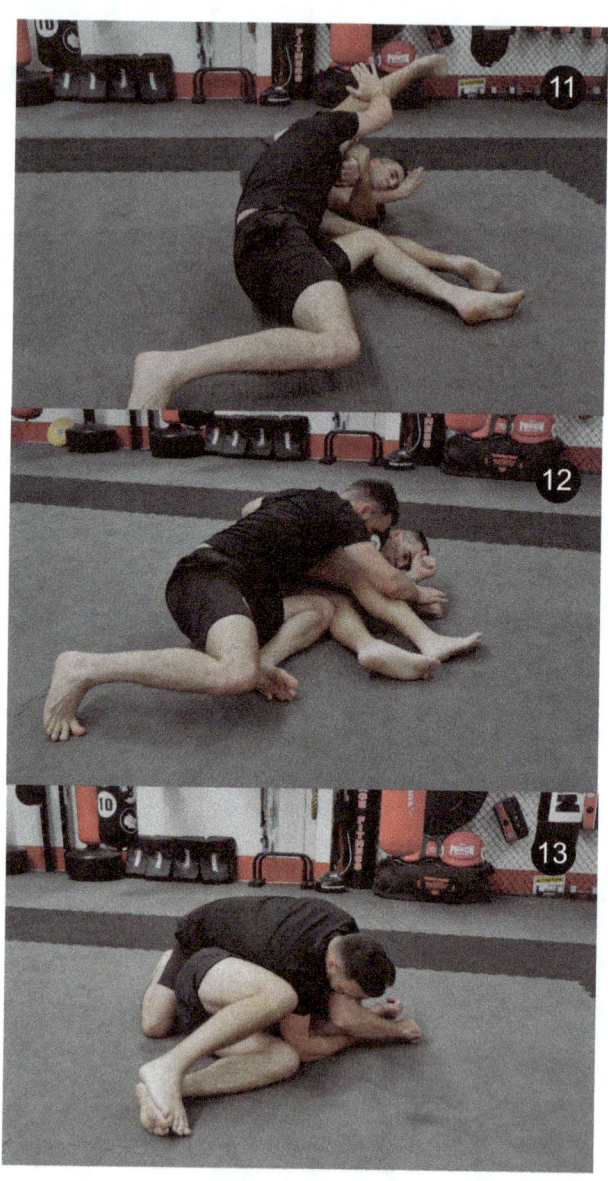

Transitions

GUARD ESCAPE

- Sitting up bring your knee in and under your opponents tail bone.

- Post your other leg out and behind at a 45 degree angle keeping one hand on the hip and the other on the knee

- As you stand up twist out and back maintaining pressure on the hip and knee this will break the closed guard

Transitions

Transitions

Transitions

MOUNT ESCAPE

- Once you have been mounted use your forearm as brace and push your opponent back till they reach your hips, you may have to hip escape a little bit.

- Bring your feet up to your hips then push your hips as high as you can throwing your opponent forward.

- As they put their hands out to break their fall reach up and secure one of their arms with a gabble grip.

- Pull your grip down to your chest trapping the arm on your body

- Now perform the "Bridge turnover" rolling over your shoulder at 45 degree angle into a guard position

Transitions

Transitions

Transitions

Transitions

SIDE CONTROL ESCAPE

- In side control bottom brace your opponent with your forearms (not your hands to prevent injury) across the hip and neck and bring feet up to your hips

- Bridge your opponent backwards at a 45 degree angle

- Lower your hips down simultaneously bring your closest knee across your opponents torso

- Gain control of the back of the head and bring your other leg up high on the back preventing the to stand up

- With a pushing pulling motion recover a full guard

Submissions

Submissions

Submissions

Submissions

TOP TRANSITIONS

- Starting in mount bring one foot across your opponents belly in a windshield wiper motion

- Keeping your shin across the belly post your other leg out at a 45 degree angle to knee on belly. Maintain control of their shoulders

- On the same side as the posted out leg bring the same hand under the opponents head

- Bring both knees into the side of their body and gabble grip your hands to finish in side control

- Bring your hand from under the head back towards you and grip the triceps and lift their shoulder off the ground

- Post up your leg closest to your opponents head out to a 45 degree angle

- Shoot your rear leg between your opponent and your posted leg finishing in scarf hold

- Repeat on the opposite side

Submissions

Submissions

Submissions

Submissions

The top 5 submissions in professional MMA make up approximately 80% of all submission wins, they are as follows:

>REAR NAKED CHOKE : 37.2%
>THE GUILLOTINE : 17.8%
>THE ARM BAR : 14.7%
>THE TRIANGLE CHOKE : 6.4%
>THE HEAD AND ARM CHOKE : 6%

This is reason a small amount of submissions make up so much is related to whats called the *"Pareto Principle"*, this means 80% of consequences come from 20% of the causes. This economic principle is found through almost every area of life including Mixed Martial Arts.

Submissions

ARM BAR

- Starting with knee on belly, control your opponents shoulders to prevent them escaping and maintain pressure on them.

- As your opponent begins to defend the knee on belly by pushing the knee off themselves place your closest hand under their tricep and grip firmly

- Pulling your opponents triceps tightly to your chest and lifting their shoulders off of the ground

- Holding the arm in close to your chest step around the head with your leg that is posted up and place your your foot under the lifted shoulder

- Sit in close to your opponent and maintain control of the trapped arm

- Lay back pulling the arm to hyper extend the elbow and ensure that the opponents thumb is pointed up to the sky

- Squeeze your knees together as you push your hips to the sky

Submissions

Submissions

Submissions

Submissions

ARM BAR ESCAPE

- Take your thumb that is pointed up to the sky and point it above your own head creating a bend in your arm.

- Step your inside leg and step over your outer leg as you turn onto your belly

- Reaching and pulling up on your opponent regain position in this case side control

Submissions

Submissions

GUILLOTINE

- Starting in a closed or open guard stretch out your arm above your head placing your hand on the ground

- Use your stretched out arm to help lift you up as your opposite arm shoots pass your opponents head, you may find it easier to open your guard at this point but return to a closed guard as soon as you complete this step

- Bring your arm across the back off the the neck and make a fist

- Punch your fist into the side of the neck to get in as deep as you can

- With the opposite hand reach through and grip your fist with a "Ball and Socket Grip" creating a choke

- Bring the non choking arms elbow up and over the shoulder of your opponent and the choking arms elbow down to your hip simultaneously to finish the Guillotine choke

Submissions

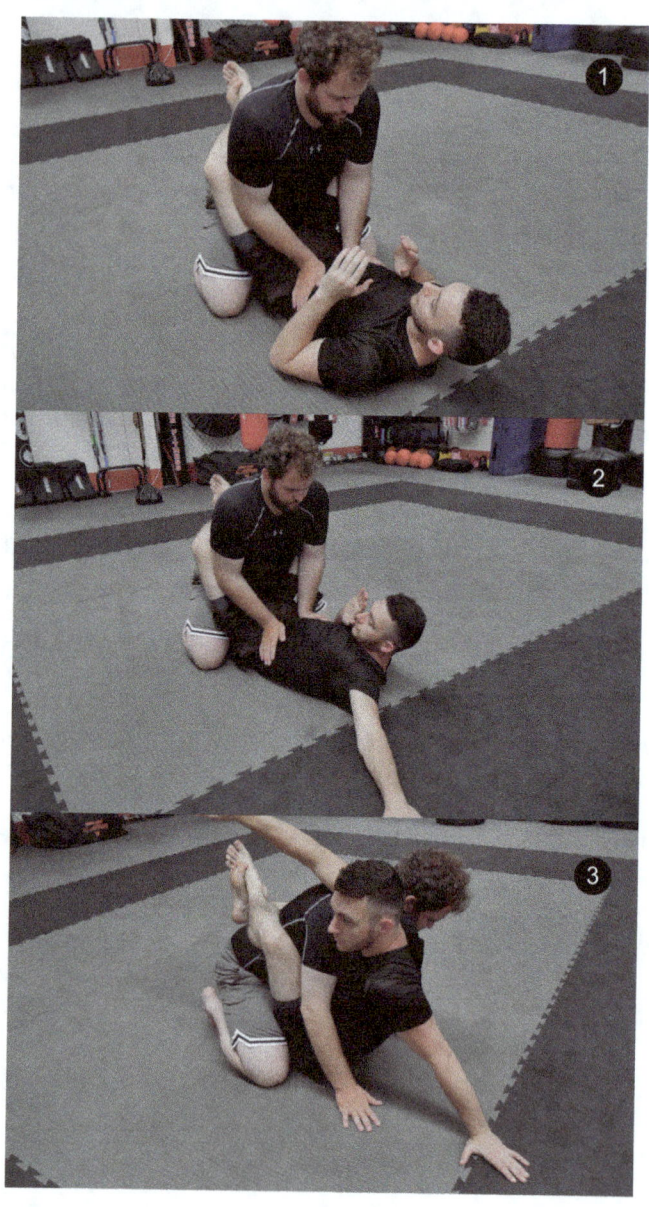

Submissions

Submissions

GUILLOTINE ESCAPE

- Before your opponent can lift the elbow over your shoulder grip the non choking arms bicep

- Stand up and push forward to nullify the choke around your neck

- Slip your hand that is on the bicep between the bicep and body of your opponent just down to your knuckles

- Keeping your hand in next to the bicep bring your elbow and wrist down to the ground

- Simultaneously lift your head up and out off the choke returning to the guard position

Submissions

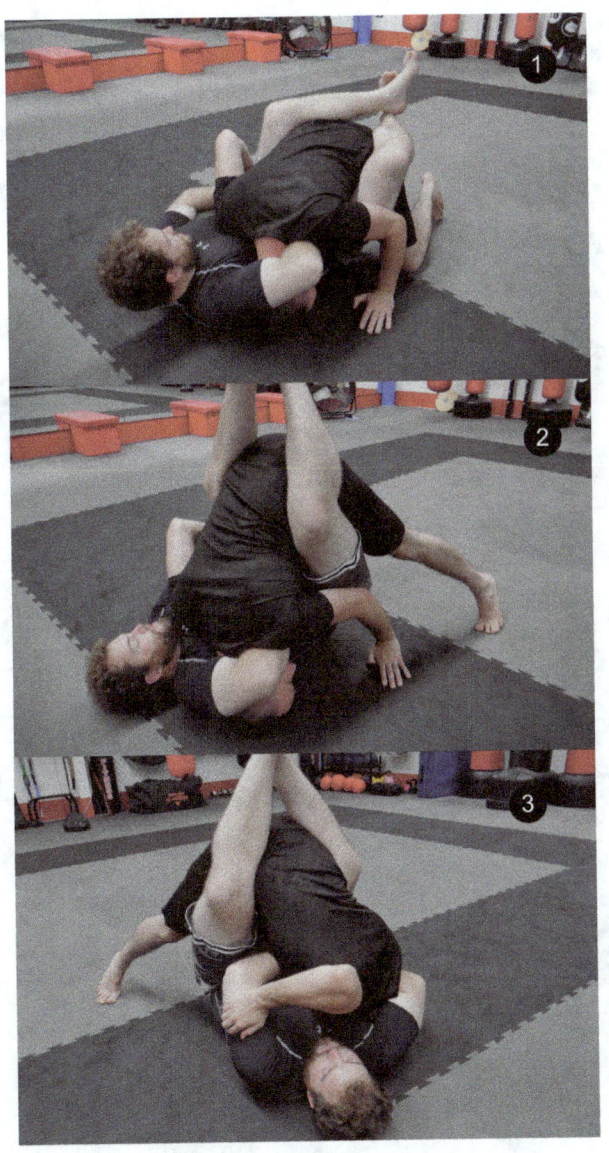

Submissions

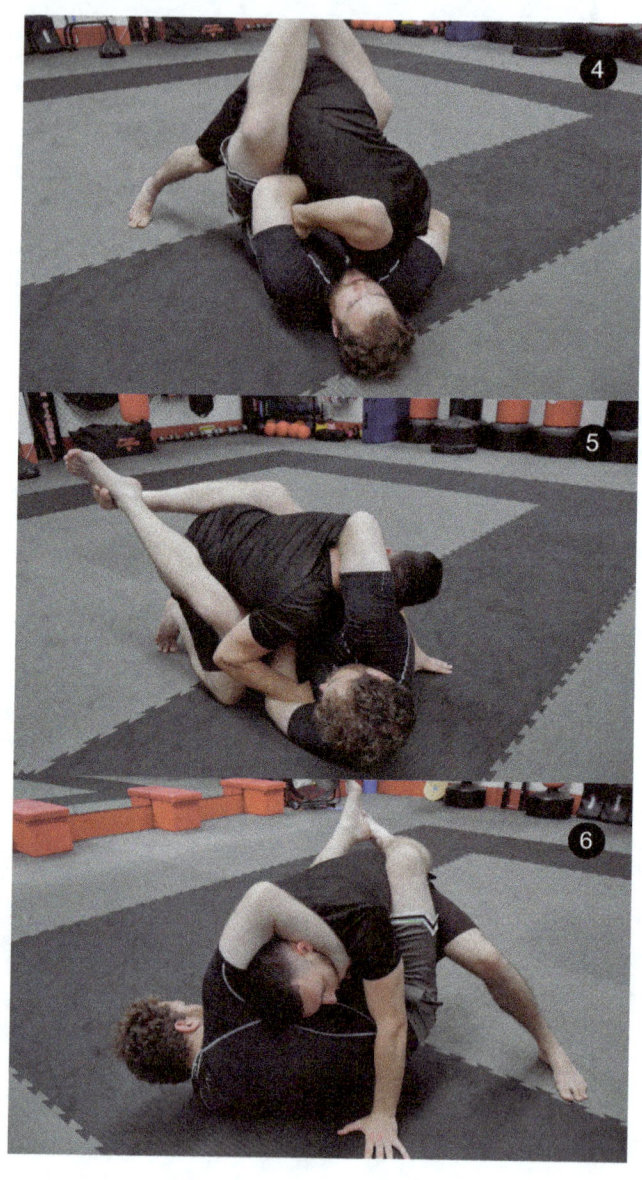

Submissions

Submissions

HEAD AND ARM CHOKE

- Starting in a scarf hold position secure the position wrapping the hand around the head and gripping your own leg.

- Push the trapped arm on your side across the neck off the opponent securing it there by pushing your head onto their head

- Release the grip on your leg and grip your other hand with a " Gabble Grip "

- Step your inside leg back between your outer leg and your opponents body

- Maintaining a tight grip lay closely besides your opponent and squeeze

Submissions

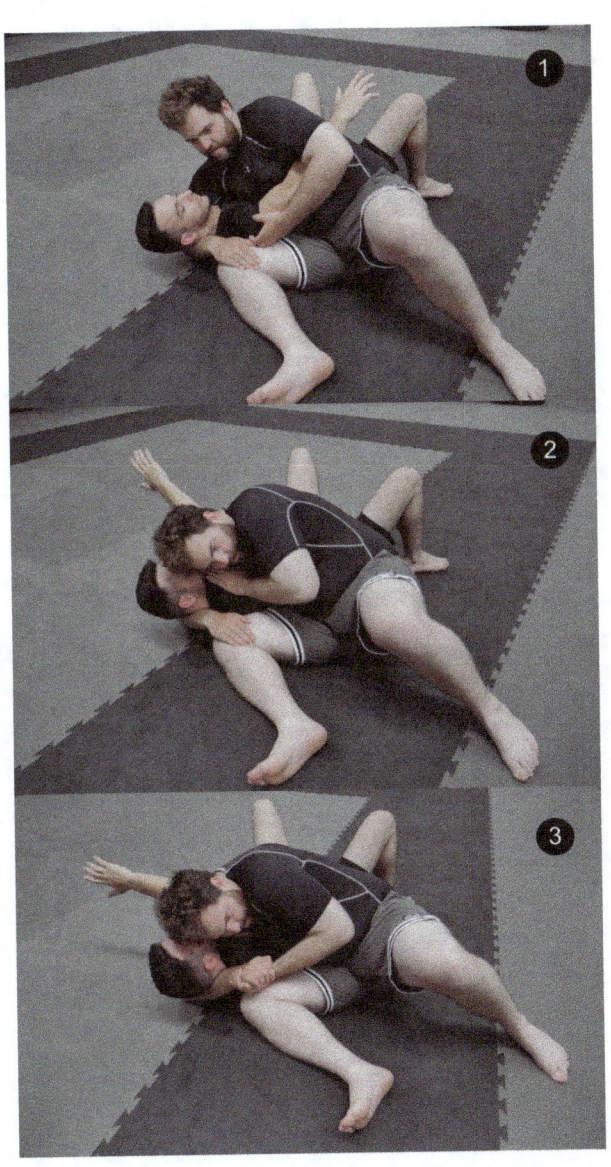

Submissions

Submissions

HEAD AND ARM CHOKE ESCAPE

- Before the choke is completed lift your far leg high into the sky

- Reach both arms up and grip behind the knee with an "S Grip"

- Maintaining a strong grip stomp your foot down to the ground lifting your head and shoulders off the ground

- With your arm that is choking you perform a backstroke motion and wrap it around the neck off your opponent.

Submissions

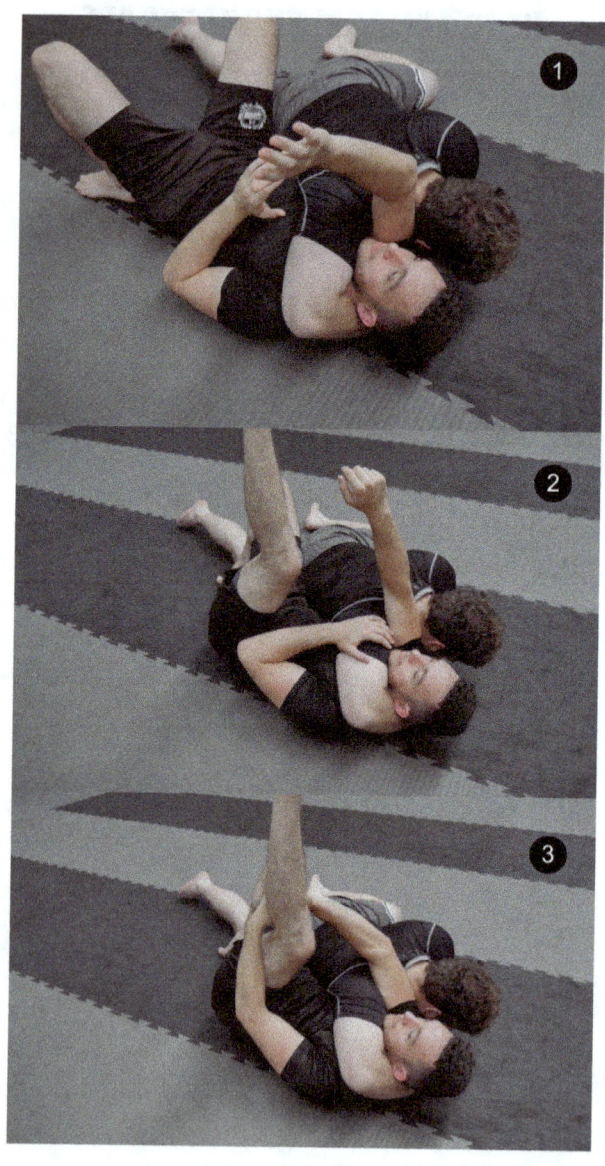

Submissions

Submissions

REAR NAKED CHOKE

- Start in a back mount with the seat belt and hooks on

- Bring the primary hand that goes over the shoulder and across the opponents chest onto the opposite shoulder gripping tight and behind the back

- Remove the secondary arm that is still under the arm of the opponent by pulling it back

- Pass the secondary hand in front of the primary hand and behind the head gripping both biceps

- Squeeze your elbows together and push them forward into the choke

Submissions

Submissions

Submissions

REAR NAKED CHOKE ESCAPE

- Ensure your head is tucked down and your shoulders are lifted up
- Reach up and behind and grip the secondary by the fingers and the forearm
- Strip the secondary arm forward, immediately trapping it between your arm and body
- Explosively bridge to the same side throwing your shoulder to the ground
- Walk your shoulders back until both of them are on the mat
- Turn in towards your opponent before they do
- You will be fighting the hands and legs in the previous steps to gain better position

Submissions

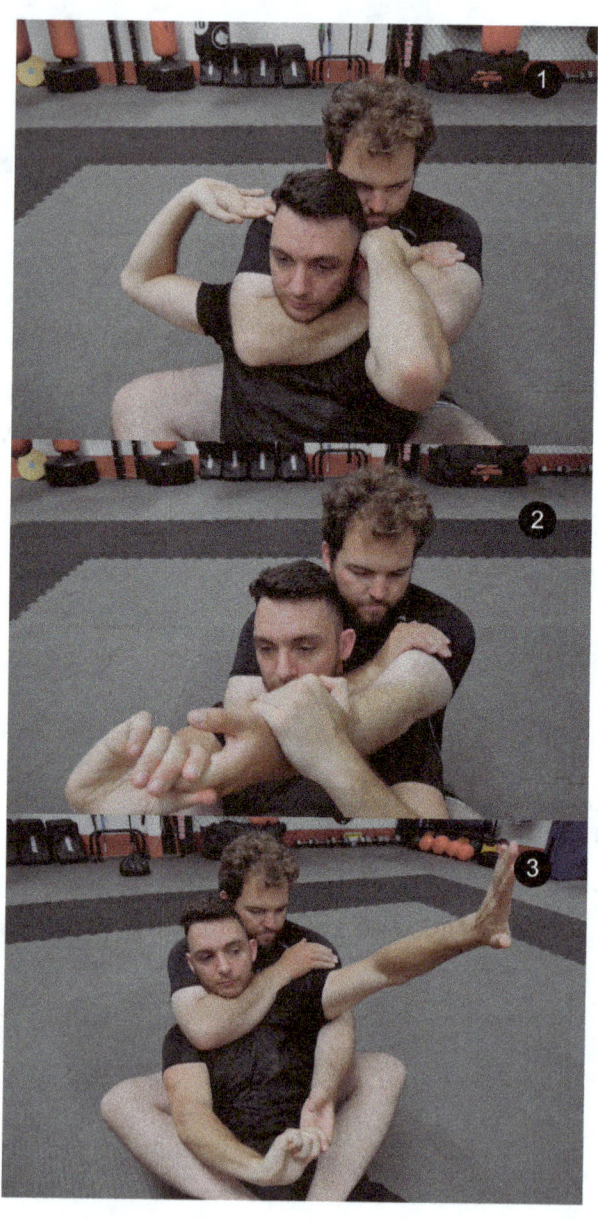

Submissions

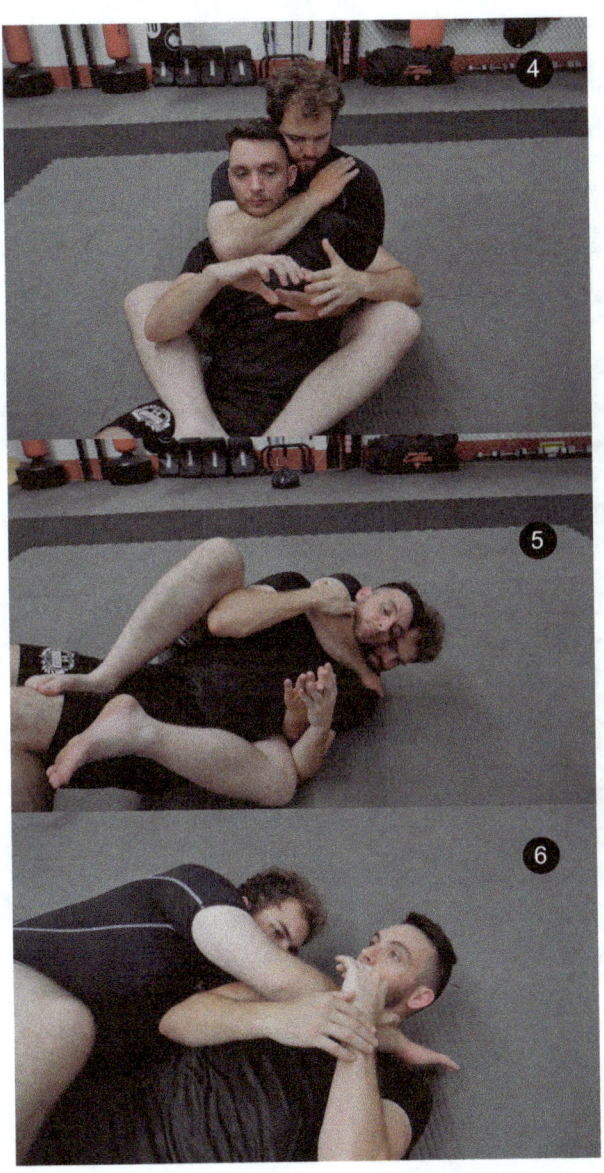

Submissions

Submissions

TRIANGLE CHOKE

- From crooked guard with one arm out, bring the other arm across your body

- On that same side the arm is now grip under the leg if your opponent

- Slightly releasing your guard pull yourself to a 90 degree angle to your opponent placing your calf on the back of their neck

- Grip the now crossed over legs shin pulling your leg down and place the opposite leg over the top locking it in place

- You should feel no gaps around your opponents neck. If you do tighten the space by ratcheting the top leg into a better position

- Control the back of the head to stop them from standing

- Shoulder walk back to the starting position whilst stretching them out

- Pull the head down and push your hips to the sky to finish

Submissions

Submissions

Submissions

TRIANGLE CHOKE ESCAPE

- From the crooked guard (pre triangle) place your trapped arms forearm across the hips of your opponent

- With your free arm grip your own forearm in tight

- Fall to the side onto the trapped arms elbow

- Walk your leg behind the back of your opponent

- To release your head from the choke look directly behind you

- Recover side control

Submissions

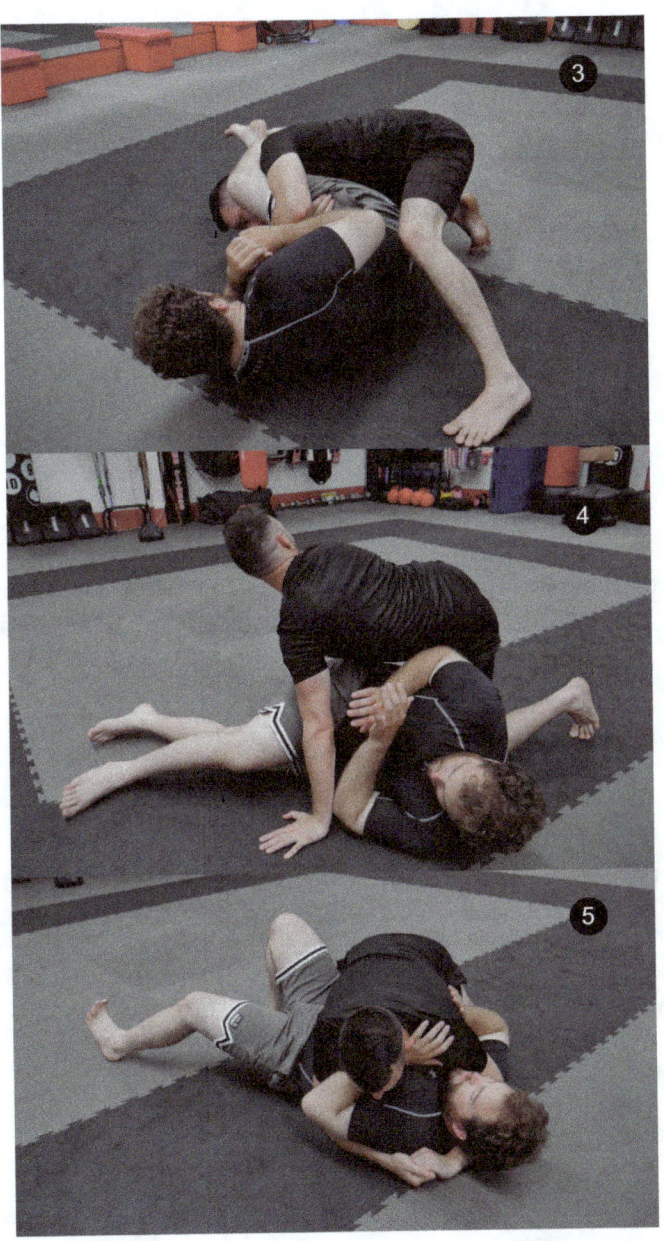

Submissions

Take Downs

The top 3 take-downs in professional MMA according to www.mmafightdb.com who did a study of 799 MMA fights and counted over 2072 trips and throws have found results that are as follows:

THE DOUBLE LEG TAKEDOWN : 38.51%
THE SINGLE LEG TAKEDOWN : 17.04%
THE OUTSIDE LEG TRIP: 10.38%

This is reason a small amount of take-downs make up so much is related to whats called the *"Pareto Principle"*, this means 80% of consequences come from 20% of the causes. This economic principle is found through almost every area of life including Mixed Martial Arts.

Submissions

DOUBLE LEG

- From your fighting stance change levels by squatting down. Keep your back straight, head up and arms tucked in tight

- Take a penetrating step forward, your front leg stepping between your opponents and your rear leg on the outside

- Simultaneous to step 2 drive your shoulder into the bladder of your opponent with your head on the outside and grab behind the knees

- As you stand up pull both your opponents legs to the side on which your head is and push with your shoulder and head into the body to the opposite direction

- Follow them to the ground and gain position

Submissions

Submissions

Submissions

OUTSIDE LEG TRIP

- From your fight stance change levels by squatting

- Perform a shoot as your front knee drives forward onto the ground

- Keep your head up, your back straight, arms in tight and aim your head to the outside of your opponent

- Wrap your now front leg around the front leg of your opponent trapping it from moving back

- Grip behind the knees and drive forward

- Follow them to the ground and gain position

Submissions

Submissions

Submissions

SINGLE LEG

- If you have an orthodox stance (Left leg forward) and your opponent is a southpaw (Right leg forward) or vice versa both lead legs are mirrored opening up for a single leg takedown

- Change levels and step off to a 45-90 degree angle towards your opponent

- Whilst stepping through pick up the front leg of your opponent under the thigh and hug it to your chest and place your ear onto the body of your opponent holding tight

- Push them forward to take them off balance

- Now taking big steps turn in towards them pulling them around and down to the ground

- Follow them to the ground and gain position

Submissions

Submissions

Submissions

MMA 8

The MMA Combo is a fundamental drill for understanding the bodies movements and the techniques you will come to learn in your MMA journey.

You can practice solo or with a partner to master these techniques.

Starting Stance

Side A   Side B

Fight stance   Fight stance

MMA 8

1 Count

Side A | Side B

Parry the jab | Jab

2 Count

Side A · · · · · · · · · · · · · · Side B

Slip the cross · · · · · · · · · Cross

3 Count

Side A   Side B

Weave   Lead Hook

4 Count

Side A | Side B

Block uppercut | Rear uppercut

5 Count

Side A	Side B
Rear leg low kick	Lead leg check

6 Count

Side A   Side B

Abosrb Kick   Lead leg front kick

7 Count

Side A

3 point block

Side B

High rear leg round house kick

MMA 8

8 Count

Side A

Sprawl on takedown

Side B

Shoot takedown

MMA FLOW 1

- As your opponent shoots for a take down sprawl out and off to an angle

- Once 90 degrees to your opponent put a seat belt on with a gabble grip

- Come around to the back keeping your arms in tight

- Place your knee in front of your opponents

- Tuck your chin and roll forward off to a 45 degree angle

- Rolling into a back mount with the seat belt still on hook your legs on the inside of your opponents

- Turn your thumb down on your primary arm (choking arm) and and then turn it up using your forearm to pry under the chin of your opponent

- Grip the opponents shoulder with the primary arm

- Pull the secondary arm back and cross it over the primary hand and behind the neck of your opponent

- Gripping both biceps with each hand use the secondary arm to push their head forward into the choke and squeeze your elbows together

MMA 8

MMA 8

MMA 8

MMA FLOW 2

- Shoot on your opponent performing the outside leg trip take down

- Jump immediately into side control and avoid their guard

- Place your forearm across the hip off your opponent and slide your knee in front of across the belly

- Once you have gained knee on belly control the shoulders so the opponent cannot roll out

- Once the opponent begins to push the knee off their belly with your palm facing upwards grab under the tricep.

- Pull their shoulder off the ground and their bicep in tight to the chest

- Step your posted leg around the head and under the lifted shoulder of your opponent

- Maintain control of the arm and sit down close to your opponent

- With one leg under the shoulder and the other across the neck lay back

- Point the thumb of your opponent up towards the sky and push your hips up hyper extending the shoulder and elbow

MMA 8

MMA 8

MMA 8

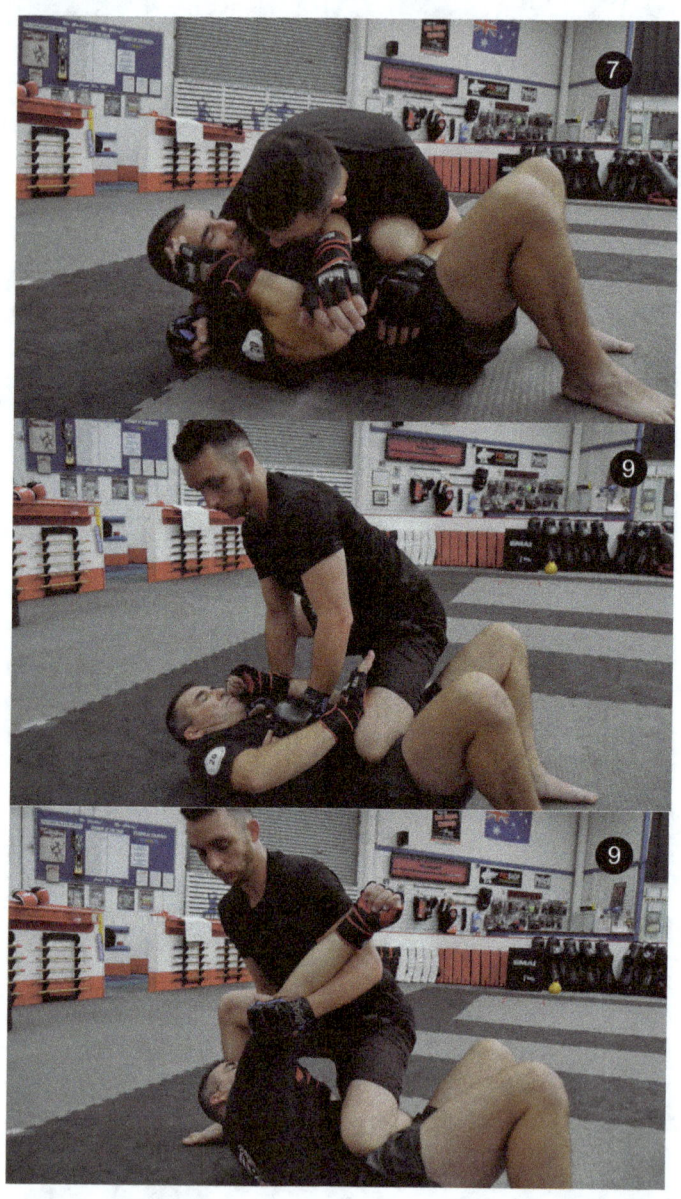

MMA 8

Fitness

Fitness

RUNNING

Running can improve oxygen uptake in the lungs and heart which can aid in physical endurance of athletes. It is a highly aerobic activity that burns both fatty acids and carbohydrates for energy which will benefit you in your mixed martial arts journey

Fitness

SKIPPING

A 2013 study from the American Association for Health, Physical Education and Recreation found that men who did 10 minutes of skipping daily for 6 weeks improved their cardiovascular fitness just as much as men who did 30 minutes of jogging for the same time period.

Because of the coordination and body awareness required of the top and bottom half of the body you are less likely to sustain injury.

Fitness

COLD EXPOSURE

A 2016 Pubmed Central study of cyclists who completed a 60 minute workout followed by 10 minutes of cold water immersion showed better results of recovery to those who passively rested for that time period.

According to www.xptlife.com/chillingout the core benefits of cold exposure are as follows:
- Boosts Human Growth Hormone

- Boosts Immune system (up to 300%)

- Increases testosterone in men (up to 490%)

- Increases sperm count

- Increases circulation

- Reduces swelling in joints

- Burns brown fat (adipose) in body

- Nor-epinephrine increases (up to 200-300%)

Fitness

HEAT EXPOSURE

In 2007 the Journal of Science and Medicine in Sport conducted a clinical trail on the effects of post workout sauna use on male runners and their endurance performance. Showing that regular sauna use increased their time to exhaustion by 32%.

According to www.xptlife.com/6-research-backed-benefits-to-sauna-for-the-athlete sauna use can:
- Sauna time can improve longevity

- Saunas can improve endurance and aerobic capacity

- Saunas can stimulate muscle growth

- Saunas can be good for the brain

- Saunas can cleanse the skin

- Saunas post-workout can boost the immune system

Fitness

RECOVERY

It is important to rest passively by taking time to relax and actively. Active recovery is quite simply low intensity exercise that keeps your blood flowing through your body which helps your muscles rebuild and recover. www.Healthline.com/health/active-recovery states the benefits of active recovery include:
- Reduces lactic acid build up in muscles

- Eliminates toxins

- Keeps muscles flexible

- Reduces muscles soreness

- Increases blood flow

- Helps you maintain your exercise routine

On your days off consider the following forms of active recovery to allow your body time to heal:
- Yoga

- Walking

- Swimming

- Cycling

- Myofascial release with a foam roller

Fitness

STRENGTH AND CONDITIONING

BICYCLES

- Lay on your back on the ground
- Place your hands on your ears and lift you head and shoulders off the ground
- Bring your left elbow to your right knee slowly
- Keep your left leg straight out and off the ground
- Repeat slowly on the opposite side

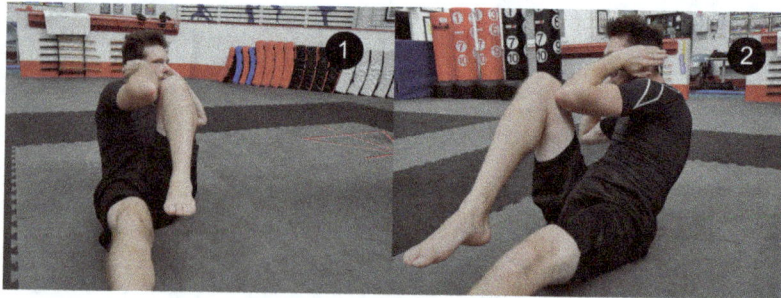

Fitness

BURPEES

- From a standing position sprawl back till your hands and feet are touching the ground

- Perform a push up

- Jump your legs up to your hands

- Jump up in the air

- Repeat

Fitness

DEADLIFTS

- Stand shoulder width apart with your feet facing slightly out

- Keep your head up and you back straight

- Sit down until the weight touches the ground

- Push up using your heel and both edges of the front of your foot

- Keep your head up and a straight back the whole time

- Repeat

Fitness

LUNGES

- With a your head up and your back straight step forward until your knee is over your toes

- Your other leg stays in the same spot as the knee dips down and almost touches the floor

- Stand back up to your original position and repeat on the opposite side

Fitness

BALL THROWS

- Hold your weighted ball in-front of your chest

- Step your left leg behind your right leg

- Step your right leg in-front of your left leg turning to a 90 degree angle

- Push off your left leg turning your hips forward and your left foot also to the 90 degree angle

- Throw the ball with your left hand using the momentum from the steps and hips turning

- Repeat on the opposite side

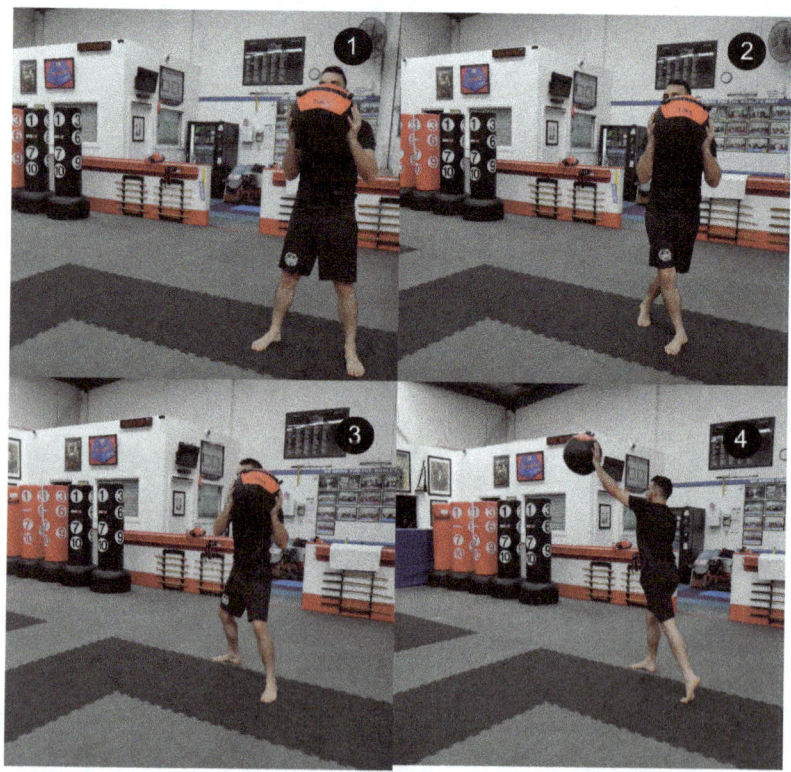

Fitness

LOW PLANK

- Hold your self up with your forearms and feet
- Keep your elbows under your shoulders
- Keep a flat back
- Engage your core

LOW PLANK ONE LEG

- Lift on leg off the ground
- Maintain a flat back
- Repeat on the other side

LOW PLANK ONE LEG ONE HAND

- Lift one leg off the ground
- Lift the opposite arm off the ground and hold it our in front of you
- Maintain a flat back
- Repeat on the other side

Fitness

Fitness

PLYOMETRIC SQUATS

- With your feet shoulder width apart sit down
- Keep a your head up and your back straight
- Explosively push off the ground jumping in the air
- Bend your knees as you land to soften the impact
- Repeat

Fitness

PULL UPS

- Keep your back straight head up and core engaged
- Pull your self up
- Slowly let yourself down
- With out your feet touching the ground repeat

Fitness

PUSH UPS NORMAL

- Start on your hands and feet with your hands under your shoulders
- Keep your elbows in tight against your body
- Keep a flat back and lower your self down
- Push your self back up
- Repeat

PUSH UPS PLYOMETRIC CLAP

- Start as you would with a normal push up and lower your self to the ground
- Explosively push up lifting your upper body from the ground
- Clap your hands
- Place your hands back to the ground
- repeat

PUSH UPS PLYOMETRIC SUPERMAN

- Start as you would with a normal push up and lower your self to the ground
- Explosively push up lifting your hands and feet off the ground
- Stretch your arms out in front
- Place your hands and feet back to the ground
- repeat

Fitness

STRETCHING

Adding Static Stretching to the end of your workout can help your muscles recover quicker and prevent injury.

Here we go through different static stretches you can add to your post workout recovery.

Fitness

HIP FLEXOR STRETCH

Fitness

HIP FLEXOR AND QUADRICEPS STRETCH

Fitness

INSTEP AND SHIN STRETCH

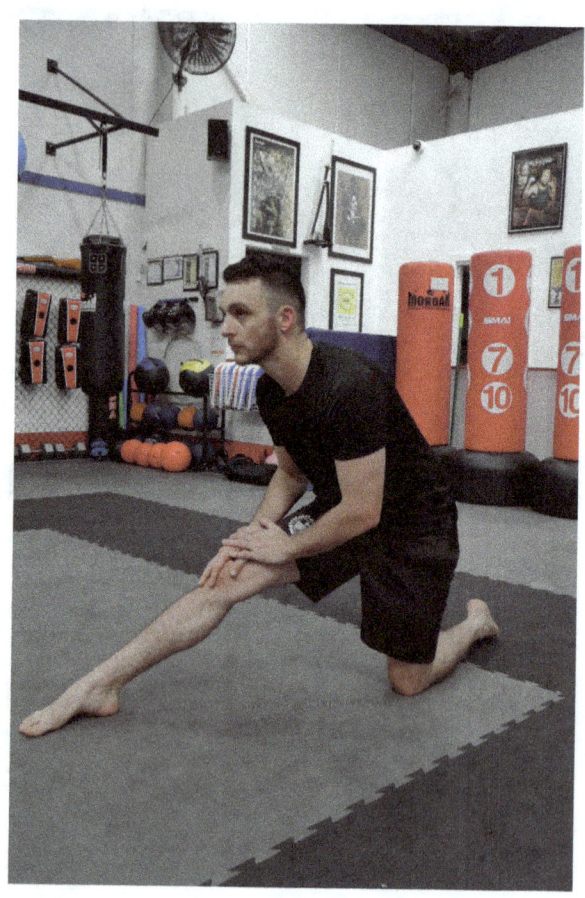

Fitness

LOWER BACK STRETCH

Fitness

HIP OPENING STRETCH

Fitness

GLUTES STRETCH

Fitness

QUADRICEPS AND KNEE STRETCH

Fitness

TRICEPS AND LATISSIMUS DORSI STRETCH

Fitness

NECK STRETCH

Fitness

STANDING QUADRICEPS STRETCH

Fitness

SHOULDER, UPPER BACK AND CHEST STRETCH

End Note

Thank you for investing in this book and most of all thank you for the invesment in your self. Whether you are looking to fight in the cage or just get fit and healthy i'm sure this will add to your journey and to the lives of people around you. Health and wellbeing is always a great investment.

As a final thought, if you find it hard to learn new things just remember to adopt a growth mindset. You can always learn new skills and you are not defined by your failures but by the effort you are willing to put in.

Fitness

Special Thanks

Soke Gary Johnson - Owner of Munen Muso Martial Arts Australia

Kyoshi Leanne Johnson - Co-Owner of Munen Muso Martial Arts Australia

Jason "Bear" Moore - Model & BJJ Coach

Sensei Liam Murray - Model & Karate Instructor

Sensei Connor Hextel - Model & Karate Instructor

Shayne McLaren - Model, Student & Taekwondo Instructor

Dean Russel - Photography

Jason Rennie - Formatting and Layout

Nina Stevenson - Wife & Biggest Supporter

Index

Index

3 Finger Hold 48

3 Point Block 40

A

Arm Bar 97

Arm Bar Escape 101

B

Back Escape 76

Ball & Socket Grip 51

Ball Throws 168

Base Stand ups 63

Body Block 37

Bridge Turnover 65

Burpees 165

C

Chest Stretch 186

Closed Guard 54

Crooked Guard 55

Cross 29

Index

D
- Dead lifts 166
- Double Leg 129

F
- Fist 26
- Frame and Evade 46

G
- Gabble Grip 49
- Glutes Stretch 181
- Guard Escape 81
- Guillotine 103
- Guillotine Escape 106

H
- Half Guard 56
- Head and Arm Choke 110
- Head and Arm Choke Escape 113
- High Guard 36
- Hip Escape 68
- Hip Flexor Stretch 176
- Hip Opening Stretch 180

Index

    Hook 31

    Hook Block 37

I

    Instep and Shin Stretch 178

J

    Jab 27

    Jiu-Jitsu 10

K

    Knee on Belly 57

    Knees 23

L

    Leg Check 39

    Low Plank 169

    Lower back stretch 179

    Lunges 167

M

    MMA 8 139

    MMA Flow 1 149

    MMA Flow 2 153

    MMA Stance 10

Index

Mount 58

Mount Escape 84

Muay Thai 11

N

Neck Stretch 184

O

Open Guard 53

Outside Leg Trip 132

Overhand Block 38

P

Parry 36

Plyometric Squats 171

Pull 43

Pull ups 172

Push Ups 173

Q

Quadriceps Stretch 177, 182, 185

R

Rear Naked Choke 116

Rear Naked Choke Escape 119

Index

Round House Bat 18

Round House Snap 21

S

S Grip 50

Scarf hold 59

Shoot 70

Shoulder Stretch 186

Side Control 60

Side Control Escape 88

Single Leg 135

Slipping 42

Sprawl 72

Stabbing Front Kick 16

Strength and Conditioning 164

T

Tactical Mount 61

Tactical Standup 74

Top Transitions 92

Training Bag 8

Triangle Choke 123

Index

Triangle Choke Escape 126

Triceps Stretch 183

U

Upper Cut 33

Uppercut Block 38

W

Weaving 44

Wrestling Stance 10

Index

Index

Index

www.ingramcontent.com/pod-product-compliance
Lightning Source LLC
Chambersburg PA
CBHW050311010526
44107CB00055B/2201